T0085807

TWO MAPS OF EMERY

Other Books by Laurence Hutchman

The Twilight Kingdom
Explorations
Blue Riders
Foreign National
Emery
Beyond Borders
Coastlines: The Poetry of Atlantic Canada (co-editor)
Selected Poems
Reading the Water
In the Writers' Words: Conversations with Canadian Poets
Personal Encounters

Two Maps of Emery

Laurence Hutchman

Black Moss
Press

2016

FIRST EDITION

Library and Archives Canada Cataloguing in Publication

Hutchman, Laurence, author
    Two maps of Emery / Laurence Hutchman.
ISBN 978-0-88753-566-6 (paperback)
    1. Emery (Toronto, Ont.)--Poetry. I. Title.

PS8565.U83T86 2016   C811'.54   C2016-903765-7

Cover art: Painting *Emery* by Laurence Hutchman

Author photo: Eva Kolacz-Hutchman

Design: Karen Veryle Monc

Black Moss Press

EST. 1969

Published by Black Moss Press
2450 Byng Road
Windsor, ON N8W 3E8 Canada

www.blackmosspress.com

Black Moss books are distributed in Canada and the U.S. by Fitzhenry & Whiteside. All orders should be directed there.

Black Moss Press acknowledges the support of the Canada Council for the Arts and the Ontario Arts Council for its publishing program.

ONTARIO ARTS COUNCIL
CONSEIL DES ARTS DE L'ONTARIO

Canada Council   Conseil des Arts
for the Arts   du Canada

PRINTED IN CANADA

*I would like to dedicate this book to the people of Emery
and to my parents*

Acknowledgements
  Some of the poems in this collection have been
published in *The Fiddlehead, The Antigonish Review,
Pottersfield Portfolio, The Nashwaak Review, That Sign of
Perfection, Canadian Author, The Commorant* and *The Emery
Village Voice.*
  A number of these poems have been previously
published in *Foreign National,* (Agawa Press, 1993) *Emery*
(Black Moss Press, 1998), *Selected Poems,* (Guernica Press,
2007) and *Personal Encounters* (Black Moss Press, 2014) and
revised. I have chosen to include these poems in this book
because they comprise a distinct collection and reflect my
experience of Emery.
  I would like to thank my publisher, Marty Gervais
and the Ontario Arts Council for a Writers' Reserve grant.
Emery Village BIA for their support: Tim Lambrinos,
Sandra Farina and Sean Delaney and many thanks to Nina
Silver and her students of Emery Collegiate Institute. I
also express my gratitude to Marion Russell (Rowntree),
Jack Devins and the other people of Emery who shared
their stories. I would most of all like to thank Eva Kolacz-
Hutchman for refined editing of this collection of poems,
for her dedication and abiding love.

Table of Contents

History of Emery

*You know, there are two pictures of Emery
—what you see today and the place where we lived.*

Jack Devins, Emery farmer

Emery Village

Two Maps of Emery

Open the book and find the map of Emery,
find the village which no longer exists,
the lots of the original settlers.
Trace the pattern of their settlement,
their lots and their concessions:
the Devins came with Governor Simcoe,
Crossons trekked by horse from Pennsylvania,
Rowntrees and Watsons emigrated from England,
Duncans and Griffiths from Ireland.

Examine the modern map of Emery
circa 1948, the year of my birth.
Look at the lines on the map,
how they lead beyond the page
into the fields and orchards I knew,
to barbed wire fences that I climbed.

Turn the pages to discover the history of the village.
Look at the buildings on the map
drawn by Marion Rowntree in the 1940's:
the blacksmith shop, the carriage shop,
the shingle mill, the community hall.
Look for the general store, the stable,
the post office and the railway station.
Find the Methodist church and Emery Public School.

Who are these farmers that plowed the fields
their tractors navigating the warm sea of wheat?
Who are the soldiers whose names are
                engraved on the monument?
What stories are hidden under the fading lines of this stone?
Whose faces are in the photo of Emery Public School?
Who lived in the abandoned houses that I explored?

During the late fifties our lives intersected briefly.
I watched farmers leaning on fences,
neighbours talking about their work.
Slowly new roads and houses rose on subdivision grids;
the farmers' fences broke and fields faded,
the end of a silent film.

For years I've been away,
yet their houses have haunted my dreams.
The farmers' voices said, "Turn from your work.
Return to a place that is no longer there."
I dream of a clear river that flows through Emery,
of a tree that grows through school windows.
"Journey" say the voices, "to find your history.
Here is the place you are looking for."

The Farmhouse

That first fall we climbed toward the farmhouse
at the top of Emery hill. Near the ravine ridge
we entered the wooden hut and
looked down into the well,
wondering where the water came from.

When my friend Les and I looked up at the house
the farmer and his dog were bearing down on us;
we turned and ran down the hill through the marsh,
with the dog chasing us, and the farmer waving his shotgun,
shouting "Stay off my land."

Months later, still afraid of that man
we walked again toward the then deserted farmhouse.
Over rusty mattresses we crawled,
sneaked past the wrecked Studebaker,
we opened the door—
child anthropologists entering an ancient tomb.

Inside the house was intact:
coal oil lamps, mirrors, a wash stand, doilies,
a church calendar "God Bless Our Home."
It was as though they had just moved out.

We opened a small black trunk, a treasure chest
and found copies of *The Globe and Mail*
going back to the beginning of the war,
and in the wind I hear
Walter Cronkite's deep voice speaking of the Battle of Arnhem.

Turning the yellowed pages
I thought of the man overseas
as I read headlines—Stalingrad, Normandy, El Alamein,
and studied photos of Churchill and Roosevelt,
resembling old trading cards.

The next week, in the cold November chill,
I saw this black trunk in the Gulfstream schoolyard,
the broken chest spilling out its papers
like calendar pages in an old movie,
clinging to the wire of the Frost fence.

A few months before families were still out
doing the wash, pumping water, feeding animals
and then they were gone.
Only the mouldy smell of mattresses,
rust stained refrigerators
and the ruined walls of the farmhouse remained,
and the memory of that nameless farmer
like an old god guarding the hilltop.

The Pump

As I was listening to the farmer Charlie Grubbe talk
about the old Emery schoolhouse pump
slowly in pieces the memories come back.

In the hot late August afternoon,
when I was picking pears from the farmer's orchard
and putting them into a wicker basket,
                  I saw the rusty pump
with its broken wooden base.

Pumping it up and down,
I hear a groan,
        a drawing sound
from somewhere deep in the earth,
then the sound of rising water
gushing out in spurts.

I cup water in my palms
to taste it,
splash it on my face,
open my eyes through dust
to see again:
the school, the football field
with the sagging uprights,
the grey gravestones leaning
beyond the waving wheat.
Here I'm standing
ten years old again in the full sunshine,
at the crossroads of Emery.

The Abandoned Church of Emery

The church was empty
no pews or Bibles,
inside the smooth concrete floor
was cool as a hockey arena in summertime,
broken stained glass panes
were lying on the floor
along with rectangles of hopscotch
with swear words drawn by children
and big valentine hearts
with initials I tried to decode.
The pulpit was solitary,
but in cold darkness
I hear the ghost of the minister,
the choir singing hymns
as wind rustles
through chestnut trees
and broken panes of framed sky.

The Emery Schoolhouse

Our new school was not built yet,
so we took the bus to Downsview
and one morning we climbed the hill to where our bus
began its route and for a couple of minutes
we saw the country kids running in the schoolyard.
That was the last year the two-room schoolhouse was open.

In chestnut season, we wandered up to this schoolyard
with grass spiking through the cracked pavement.
The large green door was open;
we climbed the stairs into the empty classroom
with its blackboards and posters.
I wanted to know what it was like to go there
imagining the Kilmers, Mark Thorpe, Tom McCullough
sitting at their desks
and the teacher teaching different grades,
Mr. Fox sweeping up the dustbane on the wooden floors.

I descended into the basement darkness.
Behind the furnace there was a door.
What was behind that door?
A deep tunnel into the earth.

Albion Bridge

I stepped between rusty spikes and missing planks,
I had been warned about the hobo,
a rugged man with wild red hair
who lingered beneath the bridge.

My father fished from the railings
—it reminded him of salmon rivers in Ireland,
all he could hook were suckers.
Hurricane Hazel took out forty bridges
along the Humber, but this one held.
Early in the 60's we still used it
for a shortcut to the Humber Valley Golf Course.

The bridge is long gone now.
I remember how difficult it was
to get to the other side of Albion Bridge,
originally named the Musson Bridge.
In the 19th century there was Chew's Mill,
Hiscock's Inn, and a distillery
which was torched in those temperance days.

This is where John Grubb built
Albion Plank Road all the way to Bolton,
where Major Mackenzie, as a boy,
threw rotten eggs from his wagon
which burst sulphurous bombs into the river below.
This is where Albert "Fish" Mason and Aubrey Ella,
on road duty tried to straighten the curve of the hill
where nameless Chinese gardeners
worked from morning to night on furrows in fields.
This is where the salmon once ran so abundantly,
the settlers said you could walk on their backs across water.

Chestnuts

We headed north in quest of chestnuts,
the last adventure of the summer before school began.
With sticks we knocked them down,
split green leather rinds to find grey-white nuts.
Later, we would harden them in the oven,
drill the hole,
carefully thread it with shoelaces
and take them into the schoolyard
for the conker battles.

Now, poring over blank maps and concession lines,
the trees shine again on red brick houses in green fields.
At the end of our scavenger hunt
that encompassed the territory of dying farms,
I remember the tree on the Duncan farm with
window curtains blowing into the form of a girl,
and the tree on Main Street where the Kilmers
played like gnomes among the ruined farm machinery.
I remember the tree by the Riley's white house,
shimmering filaments in late August heat.

The most productive tree of all
stood between the Emery schoolhouse and the church
where we found chestnuts in the grass
and carried them to the stone war monument,
with the spikes piercing the skin on our hands,
to break the sharp shells open,
then we headed home,
with chestnuts ripening in our pockets.

At the End of the Farmer's Road

The metal gate had a "No Trespassing Sign"
and later in the spring it was unexpectedly open.
I followed the farmer's road
beyond the break in the forest
to the old road across Cook's Creek
up over the hill and the ridge
to the wide deserted field
with high barn standing in its charcoal boards
and high beams, a ruined frigate.
There was an old rusty thresher
and coils of freshly bound hay,
but no sign of the farmer.
I climbed the ramp of the doorway.
Inside the air was still, with the darkness broken
by sunlight dancing in the motes of air,
the light beam like an old cinema projector
that broke through boards of barn walls
was shining on a loft corralled in hay
perhaps still holding the outline of teenage bodies
who once kissed there.
And before me the dream
—an empty hayloft
with its spongy hay still intact.
Looking up I saw
ladder like that of an old tree house,
and I began to climb the crooked boards.
It was time to jump
and for one glorious moment
I hung in the light air,
before falling into the darkness
of the buoyant hay
at the top of the hill
at the end of the farmer's road.

Gulfstream Public School

Scoutmaster

He taught us the national anthem.
It was hard to hear his words,
his face was stitched with pink zippers,
he fought hand to hand with a German soldier
and killed him, then caught shrapnel
from a bomb, struggled on
until he dropped onto rubble.

In winter, he took us on a long trek
through Black Creek conservation area
for a war game, divided us into two groups
which we named Allies and German.

For hours we
trekked, searched for
signs in the snow—
the broken twig,
the lost Mars bar,
reading the snow,
down through brambles we moved
into imagined battle.

I don't know how long we climbed
the hills, wading waist high
through drifts of snow, looking
for the elusive enemy over
crests of snow, descending
dark brush toward black water, pushing
aside wiry fences.

We never caught each other.
The cold was our biggest enemy,
the wind on the face, the freezing feet.
Finally, at the campfire
we were kid-soldiers leaning on trunks,
socks hanging on branches like dead birds.

He ordered us into lines
for the homeward trek,
breaking into his repertoire of army songs,
"Pack up your troubles in your old kit bag,"
"Mademoiselle from Armentieres, parlez-vous?"
we were marching through the drifting snow.

The Lost Glove

For my ninth birthday I got a red first-base glove,
not red, more maroon. Moulding the pocket to my hand,
I made fantastic catches in the Melody Road schoolyard.
Suddenly I couldn't find it anywhere.
I forage rooms, trunks, the attic, wanting it to turn up.
There was rumour that Lacey threw it into the pond
at the bottom of Habitant Drive and I dreamed
of rescuing it from the sludgy, turbid depths.

My baseball summer passed without a glove.
One day, Lacey confesses defiantly.
I pushed him against the railing. I want to punch him,
but his mother pressed against the window pane was yelling,
"Leave him alone."
"He stole my glove."
He cowered in the cold wind.
I grabbed him by the neck and let him go…

This icy morning I think of that glove,
marooned deep in the earth—leather flower,
scarlet heart folded on its interlaced side
lost deep in layered glacial sand
becoming the colour of the earth, and the ink—
my own name slowly dissolving into the earth.

The Last Blacksmith in Weston

Looking for wheels to build a go-cart, Les and I
ride into Weston. Inside Wilf's Cycle and Sports
we tread the worn wooden floor with sawdust smell
reminding us of old westerns
and ask the owner about wheels:
"Maybe you should try the old guy round the corner."

We walk to the street near the railway tracks,
stepping into a barn where an old man
a thin, aged Vulcan in a shiny black apron,
the last blacksmith in Weston
was standing before a blazing forge.

"Do you know where we can get wheels?"
—hoping he has some lying among
the old harnesses and broken carriages.
He looks at two eleven-year-old boys who've
stumbled into their adolescent twilight zone.
"I could make you a wheel,
but it'd cost you more than it's worth."

Beyond the darkness of the barn we see meadows
where suddenly from the clouds
light breathes and the town lies still,
a museum with wires, railway ties
and roads stitch the world together.

Grandmothers

We would see the grandmothers of friends
from Italy or Germany draped in black:
shawls, dresses, stockings, shoes,
their bronzed faces wrinkled, with moles and facial hair
from Grimm's fairy tales.
We would see them at Italian Gardens,
trying to hold onto their granddaughters
who danced in the wind just out of their reach.
They looked at us as if we were savages of the new world.
They would arrive in summer,
sit on porches and speak in foreign languages.
Sometimes they would sniffle or wave,
but dismiss us with an uncomprehending gaze
when we would ride by on our bikes
and nod imperceptibly toward them.
If we got close enough they lightly smiled
calling out to offspring who no longer understood them.
Oma, my Dutch grandmother dressed in a neat grey suit
had become distant and silent with the years,
talked mostly with her eyes, her smile,
her hands reaching awkwardly toward me…

The Fathers

The fathers of our streets were quiet
when they weren't working or drinking,
until they broke out in rage.
When David acted out the Howdy Doody puppet show
his father brooded like a dictator,
then kicked us out into the cold spring air.
Kenny let us play in the loft of his barn,
we climbed up to a diving platform
jumping and gliding into engulfing straw.
In the Victorian house his father shouted,
"How many times have I told you not to disturb the
animals?" as he spun Kenny across the floor.
Richard brought us over to look at his father's birds,
his basement was converted into an aviary
—everywhere red, blue, yellow feathers.
Suddenly his father stomping down the stairs,
"What have I told you about having people over?"
Slapped his son, knocking his glasses from his face.
Richard cowered against the wire cage,
blood trickling from his nose.
The fathers were angry or silent. Mr. Bishop,
handsome like Ronald Colman,
suffered shell shock, never spoke of the war,
of the white lash scars across his back,
his fingers finding comfort only when planting
gladioli bulbs in the black earth.
The strangest father was the German,
with a house full of secrets.
When the war was ending
he had limped miles to surrender to the Allies.
Sometimes he looked at us with eyes
colder than the cobalt of a rifle barrel,
other times his eyes were those of a wounded animal.

The Toys of Johnny Wolf

He got off the school bus
holding his crutches in one hand,
stepped awkwardly down.
His shy eyes turned away,
as he limped before us
across Tumpane schoolyard.

"He broke his leg trying to fly,"
Karl, his brother, said slyly.

Later that fall Johnny brought
a hand grenade to "Show and Tell."
"Evacuate the room," ordered the kindergarten teacher
while children ran screaming down the hall.
Dumbfounded, he stood in the doorway,
wondering why everyone had deserted him.

He led me down
into the unfinished rec room,
behind the rumbling furnace,
to show me his father's collection.
I held the bronze bullets
and the hand grenade
like a small green pineapple,
a Mattel toy, only heavier.

Toronto Maple Leaf Stadium

We get off the clanging streetcars
move among the throngs of people,
vendors hawking baseball programs,
pennants, bats and other souvenirs.
We follow the ramp
that spiral among the peeling stucco walls
with vaulted windows swooped by vagrant pigeons
and we emerge into the early evening air,
the players were already warming up on the infield
throwing their deadly accurate baseballs.

I'm 12 years old with other Sunday school boys,
Mr. Upton puffs his cigar exhaling purple smoke,
speak of the strategies as if he were the coach.
There was always something happening out there
before the islands on the lake,
when the freighter's foghorn bellowed through the night,
the mysterious aroma from the malt silos
permeated the dusky air,
a biplane trailing the cryptic messages
of unknown lovers across the mauve curtain of the sky,
men in candy striped suits barking out orders
throwing bags of peanuts across the unruly fans.

It is hard to focus our attention
until the sun fades under the blue bars of evening
dissolving into the night and the lights flashes on.
The outfield becomes greener,
and light more intense on the infield.

The action draws us into
the secret codes of pitchers and catchers,
the loud judgement of umpires calling players out,
the protests of coaches.
When the player drives the ball
through the gap,
the crowd rises to the edge of its seats,
exhaling a mutual sigh.
Through memory's lens
we don't remember when or
who turned the play of the game,
maybe it was one of the best sluggers Steve Demeter
sliding into a kind of dusty glory,
to that safe plate at home
in the diamond light of the stadium on Lake Ontario.

Milkweed

A thirteen-year old boy in the ravine
lifts the milkweed pod through mauve sky upward,
releases seeds to the moon.
        The weed, not flower, not jack-in-the-pulpit,
but rough skin, nodules,
        bumps, hard metacarpal,
            faded puce, mole fur, velvet-ridged, a broken boat.
Once in public school we drew the pod
until it became a thousand things:
a clown striped banana,
a green beaked parrot perched in the wind
or a mouth opening revealing
soft down skin
            with tiny seeds that resembled
delicate Japanese prints.
The pod breaks open, launches its seeds,
humming-bird's tail, comet-blue light…
like decorations of an Irish Christmas tree.
When blowing in the wind
they dance, circles rise, spin and drop jazzy rhythms
words… rising… rushing…
        domestic sputniks,
playful gyroscopes,
            drifting stars.
At thirteen, I flip open its coarse green-tufted skin
among tall frosted grass
    they float up a ladder of lace,
  space pods
            spiralling through the mist
                toward the moon—
                their own milky way.

Black Creek Pioneer Village

I linger under the loft in the alcove of the barn,
look through the panes of the frosted window
and for a moment here
I imagine a Christmas in 1840 in York.
I could see a girl in the room
with ruffled petticoats holding her porcelain doll,
a boy in Victorian clothes kneeling over his steel toy train.
"Time to move on, students," says Mr. Smallbridge.
We climb onto the horse-drawn hay wagon
which lumbers across the dusty road of Steeles.

In Joseph Stong's big barn
I touch barley rakes, pitchforks,
feel gritty wooden surfaces of butter churns.
As I stand in the wide doorway,
a cold wind is blowing around us,
the old man talks about threshing,
"This was the way we separated wheat from chaff."
I lift up the fallen wheat,
letting it trickle in streams of golden grain,
the dusty chaff blows away, a parable of Judgment Day.

I am walking here, walking and thinking,
trying to place myself a hundred years ago,
still feeling the grain in my palm.
In the late autumn
at twilight I clamber up the hillside,
pause before a garden,
leaning on the fence
I inhale rich scents slowly, pronounce under my breath:
tarragon, thyme, sage, coriander…

Icebreakers

Spring draws us out of school
    through the subdivision
        out across fields to the hill.
        We slide down the mud runway
            into the plaster of paris ravine
                where the stream bursts its ridged banks.
    We jump over swells and ice-clefts
        mounds of dog-brown snow as
    water charges through the pipe grate;
we are on the ice one last time this year
and the world is flowing again.
My eye follows the sweeping water
    —there an otter dives and is gone
        down to the oxbow and side spit
            to where water widens at the gap
                flowing beyond forests of the peninsula.
        I hear the sound of woodwinds
            through the tinkling ice
                as currents carry suburban garbage.
    Beyond the leaning reeds
we crawl onto the edge of ice
    find crevices and ice bridges
        snap down the overhangs
    and we become icebreakers
        lumberjacks balancing on rolling logs,
      rock 'n' rollin' on the slippery edges
    singing in the spring water
until the ice cracks
and we slide down into the drink
    where water rises to our red rims and over,
      sink down into the ultimate soaker.
      (Still, when no one is looking
        you can go back to being an icebreaker).

First Desk

Late at night the sandalwood desk
moored like an old sea chest.
On this desk I wrote essays of explorers
who quested for a way to China
ending up in northern frozen shores,
wars between Aboriginals and Americans
I forgot, lost in my own child's wars.

Where did I get this desk?
The face comes back to me
of the high school student who one day
left the semi-detached life of our subdivision,
his desk and books behind,
the book of Pauline Johnson
with rhymes like canoe paddles
dipping through the darkness,
a pre-war reader with trains and planes.

I kept there the polished mother-of-pearl knife,
coins from my *Globe and Mail* route,
the Beehive NHL all star autographed photographs,
the Bible with its pale illustrations of miracles,
Genesis with the red apple of sin
next to eternal Archie, forever Jughead.
And an archive of cards: labyrinth, puzzle, World War II
Pearl Harbour, Iwo Jima—wounded soldiers,
the smell of gum in generations of baseball stars
of the National and the American Leagues.

Where is the desk now?
It was gone so long ago,
just gone when we moved
and nothing came with us.
I didn't even notice until now,
the lost bureau open once more, waiting.

A Young Girl Called Noreen

In the middle of the grade eight class
she sat silently beside me.
She wore a twilight blue sweater.
After Christmas and the holidays,
she did not come back, although I expected her to.
Just before "God Save the Queen" and the "Lord's Prayer"
the teacher said
"I have terrible news, class.
Noreen Gaughan passed away during the holidays."
Yes, that's probably what he said.
The sound of her name reminded me of a skipping song.
"On the mountain stands a lady
who she is I do not know."
I looked over at her empty inkwell.
I thought of her brother, Douglas.
I think they may have been twins
and I walked up to him and said,
"I'm sorry about your sister."
He looked at me and smiled.
I saw how much they looked alike.
I remember her silence as a warmth,
        how it moved on the air,
her words quiet as spring water.

Playing Hockey on Crang's Pond

We dreamed of playing at the Maple Leaf Gardens,
waited for *Hockey Night in Canada* following
The Plouffe Family and *Don Messer's Jubilee*,
and the chorus of the Esso commercial
What a great, great feeling,
what a wonderful sense
of pure enjoyment and of confidence...

At the end of the fifties
the place to play hockey was at Crang's Pond.
We played with the Wolf brothers, Upton and Ritch
tightening skates on the frozen banks
striding onto the ice, clearing the rink and choosing sides.

Each game was different:
the swerves, the dekes, glides, passing and shooting
to break through the defense,
bearing down on the goalie
(the way I saw Béliveau or Mahovlich move)
aiming for a corner by the boot post into the snow net.
After the breathy exhaustion of the sudden death goal
we left our indecipherable signatures on the dark ice.

We always tried to prolong the hockey season
despite the water lapping the reedy pond's edge
and the ice splitting not far from us,
getting softer, turning a little gold.
Taking off our coats and gloves
we played the game into the warm afternoon until
the whole damned pond sagged and cracked beneath us.

Miss Kristopherson's Writing Club

She sat on the corner of the desk
wearing a tight black dress
with her long legs in black stockings
and her hair tumbled like that of a movie star.
In grade eight extracurricular activities
I gave up basketball and volleyball
to join the school newspaper.
When she asked me to find a story
I interviewed the players
after our victory on the ice.
As she read my writing
I looked at the freckles around her neck
and just above her breasts
while perfume wafted over me
like a tropical breeze.
She drove us into a kind of frenzy
like a woman from playboy foldouts.
Was there anything more powerful
than a 13 year's old fantasy of Miss Kristopherson?

The Red Nib Pen

It was a modern version of the quill
in that tradition of Shakespeare and Dickens
or the art of Chinese ideograms.
In autumnal season of grade eight,
attaching the nib to the pen,
I tried to master the art of penmanship,
the loops of the " *f* " or "*l* " or the curve of "*a*" or "*r*"
the symmetrical "*k*" or the eccentric "*q*"
with the sound of the scraping of a skater
over hard ice I was grooving the letters
onto the blue lines of the foolscap.

I copied Bliss Carman's, "Songs of a Vagabond,"
the formal treaty articles of England and America,
ending the war of 1812,
Thomas Edison's inventions,
the story of intergalactic space travel.

Then one day we put away the pens.
They were gone like the scarlet CN trains
or the passenger ships on the Great Lakes.
The next year in high school
in the factory-like typing class
the Underwood typewriters clanged
their bells at the end of every line.

Italian Gardens

On the summer weekends thousands of Italians
and the local kids converged on the old Rowntree farm.
Across from the house there was a dance floor
and a bandshell with a jukebox, and behind it,
a dressing room for the swimming pool.

The crowded terrazzo floor spun with couples.
Italian men with their new Canadian girlfriends
swirled into this rock 'n' roll fever.
Sausages on grills sputtered under bannered tents,
bachelors ate thick crusted pizza,
drank bottled Brio and licked Spumoni.
Accordions squeezed out "Volaré."
There were flags, greased pole climbers, diving clowns,
champion European cyclists in spandex circling the track,
lines of whiskered Italian grandmothers
dressed in black, staring at the dancers,
holding their granddaughters
with their puffy, out of place crinolines in check.

There were extraordinary days: Gina Lolobrigida sashayed
through the bee-humming apple orchards like the Queen
of Sheba. Bobby Curtola rock 'n' rolled
in the bandshell, NHL Allstars
Lou Fontinato, Carl Brewer, Frank Mahovlich
                    played baseball on the diamond.

Always the music emanated from the bandshell
decorated with panthers and tigers in pastel jungles.
Inside change rooms boys looked
through the knotholes at the women undressing
(warned by younger girls
who stuck pins through the holes)
as they sought a vision of breast or fiery bush.

There were young couples who sauntered
into the woods, as men with binoculars
peered like spies.
On Sunday mornings the priest celebrated Mass,
intoned Latin over the terrazzo dance floor,
atoned for the sins of the day before.

Sportsland Park

T. Alec Rigby, a deep-sea diver and lumberjack
in the early 1960's created Sportsland Park,
the largest swimming pool in the world,
so large it had to be patrolled by lifeguards on horseback.
It's gone now. No record of this place.

Before it was just a large crater that had been bulldozed
beside a forest called Maryland Gardens
and people paid 75 cents a car for entrance.
The colour of the water was dirty brown.

Because Rigby had owned a concrete company
he could afford to put all that cement into a large
swimming pool about the size of eight or ten pools.
Each year brought new attractions:
the arcade where you could practice shooting a rifle
against popup gorillas, lions and elephants
and the pinballs machines which lit up and clanged.
Trampolines were built into the ground,
a golf range and a stable to rent horses.
Rigby had bought a miniature railway
from the Tivoli Gardens in Copenhagen.

There were the days when the CHUM 1050 crew
broadcast from the trampoline area
and Bob McAdorey tossed out 45's
into a crowd of stampeding teenagers.

My friend Karl Wolf knew a way to sneak in by the back,
we had to cycle by the farmer's red brick house,
along the wooden fence and hide our bikes
under the trees near the north end,

then slip through the barbed wire fence,
circumnavigate the main entrance to get inside,
however, soon a larger fence with turnstiles appeared.

On the last day of the season I tried the high board,
my Uncle Claude drove us up.
With an autumn chill in the air
I swam out to the tower and climbed
the white steel rungs, past the second board,
looking down I could see the farmland to the north,
the cars streaming along the 400.
The great pool stretched before me
as I walked out to the end of the board
and stopped at the edge
remembering the boy who burst
his belly down at Christy Pits.
Time to let go.
I jumped out with a great feeling
of momentary suspension,
that delicious falling through the air,
down into the depths,
and I swam up surfacing through the bubbles
into the fresh sunlight. The season was over.

Next year the pool was closed.
I imagined the nearly empty place,
an aquamarine shell like the ruined baths of Caracalla,
and the water from the swamp
seeping slowly through its cracked surfaces.
It was the end of Rigby's dream.
But he had already moved onto his Ripley's museum of
        oddities
and was thinking again of buying a Mexican volcano.

Emery Collegiate Institute

Typing Class

Sitting down at my electric keyboard
I am Victor Borge of the piano
or Luis Borges alive in the storm of words.
Come, let us compose the morning.
Suddenly I'm back in my grade nine typing class,
Miss Isabel Mendizabal, enchantress of
A Thousand and One High School Nights,
is holding my fingers arched high above
unknown keys and suggested
"You have fine fingers for the piano,"
then gave me the lowest
                typing mark in the history of Emery.
A mad secretarial conductor she held the cane,
decoded the alphabet in coloured combinations
of the chemical table of elements
in the classroom where
thirty-three future secretaries
punched out keys with the precision of medical formulae:
"ASDF and now HJKL and WERT and UIOP"
using Doctor Seuss combinations again and again.
"Dog sat on the cat."
"Man ran on the moon."
"Don't look at your fingers—
look straight ahead."
The bells in the room gone wild like the music
of Mussorgsky's "Night on Bald Mountain."

French Dictation

Seeing the poster in the college hallway,
Dictée des Amériques 1994
I remember the piercing words
coming from the green plastic tape recorder,
Écoutez, *n'écrivez pas!*
—the shrill voice of a dictator from the Franco-Prussian war.
It was a voice calculated to evoke fear,
Et les poules de Monsieur Dupuis...VIRGULE,
sounds of panic, swirling turbulence,
a needle punctures the skin.
I spin like Lloyd Bridges in *Sea Hunt*
bubbles bursting around my twisted mask
drifting to the bottom of the sea
—*et puis, les poules dans le jardin*
deviennent ivres... POINT D'EXCLAMATION!
The words came fast like a fusillade.
The verbs lined up like battalions on a battlefield:
futur simple, futur antérieur, futur conditionnel...
The dictator droned on about the drunken chickens
and my pen limped across the page,
anticipating the impending red casualties...
Hitchhiking from Algeciras to Madrid,
an eccentric Moroccan threatened
to throw me into the night of the Spanish desert.
The only way to remain in the car was to speak French:
every noun, every verb, every phrase I could remember,
the works of French 101: *L'Étranger, Huis-clos*
Le Livre de mon Ami
—making up the language as I went along,
hearing the sound of the dictator's voice,
"Ecoutez, n'écrivez pas!"

Mesa forms in the desert became wolves.
Shadows of trees became bandits.

Then the language became my ally,
allowing me to stay in the safety of the car
mile after mile after mile.
And so I talked about *mauvaise foi*,
Meursault, *un autre Arabe*
Rimbaud, *le dérangement de tous les sens*
Baudelaire, *la nature est un temple.*
I told the driver it didn't matter if the car
wasn't safe, and the insurance had run out.
Then I remembered the rules,
felt the rhythm of the phrases.
I talked of the virtues of Morocco:
les grands lacs, les montagnes, la mer,
I talked about anything *sous le soleil*
just to stay in the car
just to get to Madrid…
parle de de Gaulle, parle de Québec
parle de Garde civile et parle de Franco
parle de Lorca
parle de l'amour
parle de fromage
parle de vin, de fleurs,
de Paris, de Londres
parle de la neige du Canada
mais ne parle pas en anglais.
We drove past the great fallen castles,
spoke of the words of the dictator.
Then *les mots sont mes amis.*
The car, a strange wide-finned ambulance
rumbled through the wild sea-blue Spanish night.

Train accident at Leduc, Alberta

"1808 day liner now boarding on track 2 for Edmonton."
As I look out at Calgary Stampede cowboys in the station,
the train begins its journey northward.
Beside me a young bald man introduces himself,
"I'm going to open a bank in Redwater.
What are you reading?"
"Ian Fleming's *Live and Let Die.*"

The sun sweeps a shadow over undulating hills
where a large herd of cattle grazes.
A hawk rises and falls in flight
reminding me of "The Windhover."
I close the book and stare out of the window
to the slow rhythmical motion of the pumpjacks.
I imagine the summer ahead,
hiking the mountains by Maligne Lake.

Suddenly there is a bang,
large pieces of metal
were flying past my window,
I'm thrown up against the front seat.
The train screeches to a halt.

"Why are we stopped?" asks an old lady in the corner.
The conductor opens the door and quietly says:
"The train has hit a car. There is nothing to worry about."
"Was there anyone killed?"
 asks the girl in a gingham dress.
"I don't know miss. The train has been derailed."

When I walk along the gravel
several people were looking down at
the wreck of a Pontiac under the diesel,
the driver's hands grip the wheel,
to the side among the reeds
the little body of a boy floats face down
his fingers uncurled in black water.

The conductor speaks to the engineer:
"It wasn't your fault. You did what you could."
The air was cool and dark in the compartment
when I came back.
"Whose fault was it?" asked the old lady.
The man across wearing a straw hat says
"Probably the driver's was racing with the train."
The banker smiled from his seat.
"I got some good pictures."

I cannot stay here,
I jump on the gravel
and walk a hundred yards from the train
back to the bare crossing.
Why was he in a hurry?
Maybe someone was expecting him at home.
I could see his wife, the mother of the boy.
She will remember this morning
all of her life.

When I return to the train
the rest of the passengers were gone.
Only the banker remains.
"Thought you might need your stuff."
We sit silently at the back of the bus
as it drives to Edmonton on a hot June afternoon.

Climbing The Whistlers

It was three miles from our camp
to the base of The Whistlers.
On the lower slopes
a few people were gathering mushrooms.
The summit looked remote.
Are we going to reach it this afternoon?

The day began to wear on,
I looked at the chalet against the turbulent clouds.
Its strange gold angular shape
looked like a mini acropolis.
Clambering on large round boulders,
reminding me of something in a myth
as we climbed up and over them,
moving above the ski slope.

When I paused and turned
I was shocked how high we were.
The people gathering mushrooms
were now almost indistinguishable.
We were surrounded by the range of mountains,
the Athabasca River and the lakes
looking like jade on a pendant.
 (It was a perspective that could change your life).

Up the rocky slopes,
the small acropolis began to reappear.
As we were approaching the cliffs
I wondered how we would be able to climb
to it in our running shoes
through a large field of shale
with little slabs of flat stones
and I suddenly slipped and began to slide,

kept sliding, slower and then faster.
What if I couldn't stop?
I thought of the things I could do in my life.
Ahead I saw a large rock
with an edge.
I reached for it
and held it tightly in my grip
to stop my slide.
I took a deep breath
and the large valley stilled into focus again.

Slowly I began to climb up again,
planning my path across the face of the mountain.
When we had reached the top of the ridge,
the wind was cool with snow banks
around us in the mild August air
and we savoured the moment.

Medicine Lake

I left the camp and took the road to Maligne Lake.
The sun was not yet up,
the air was as still as it had ever been
as I walked over the bridge of swirling waters
and when I raised my eyes I saw
a roe and buck standing on the embankment
and around the curve a green station wagon
slowing down and stopping.
The driver was an Aboriginal man with his grandson.
He was smoking a cigar.

"I can take you as far as Medicine Lake" he said.
"We're going to fish there…
It's a strange thing about that lake,
every fall it empties and then fills up in the spring.
The Indians say that the water has healing powers."

After 15 miles of curving roads
the grandfather said, "This is as far as I go."
I sat on the talus slope overlooking Medicine Lake,
looking at the green station speeding off.
I remembered the night in Banff under Cascade Mountain
walking among the tourists and discovering
a bookshop where I picked up a book about Freud
and for the first time read
the map of the ego and the unconscious.

I picked up small stone and threw it into the water.
I could see the Aboriginal man and his grandson
out on the boat outlined by the sunshine.
I threw another and watched the ripples
forming concentric circles,
moving out like one thought following the other.

Riding the Night Freight Train
from Jasper to Edmonton

Waiting for the 404 express
we listen to rumbling of freight cars
on the last night of our trip.
It is time to jump
and we scramble with our bags,
running alongside the train,
looking for an open car,
but there were none.
We could only reach the oil platform.

We are moving away
from the chalet on The Whistlers,
the twinkling lights of Cottonwood Campground
where we carved our names in the pine beams,
by the churning Athabasca River
and the road out to Maligne Canyon.

We hold onto the side bar
when the long curving train
is accelerating into the mountains
passing high cliffs
and leaning against the railing
like a banister before a huge theatre
we sing: "It's been a hard days' night
we should be sleeping like a log."

The mountain swallows us
and we hold onto the oil dome
as the train winds in serpentine motion,
past mountain peaks like ancient tyrants,
the violent rivers, silver eskers
under the bronze helmet of the moon.

Beyond the mountains
through the acrid smell of lumber
the train slows down
and stops at the mill town.
The guard starts to patrol the platform
as we huddle against the black dome,
his search light passes over us.

As the train accelerates through the darkness,
gliding in its sublunary flight
I try to keep awake.
The night becomes primeval,
creatures breathing in thick swamps
and the green light surreal
as I dream of crashing
into the hidden depths of the lake.

Under a pale Martian sky
the train slows down
past grain elevators and spectral towers
reaching the outskirts of the city.
It is time to jump.
A CN cop sees us
and with rolled up sleeping bags
we begin running
into the rays of the rising sun.

High Jumping

What was it that drew me to high jumping,
to that round silver bar
like a bridge between standards,
to raise my body over the barrier?
From the Eaton's carpet department
I got a bamboo pole.
Every year in the spring time we practiced jumping
with no pit or sand
and later using couch cushions.

Olympian Russia jumper, Valery Brumel
was my hero in the midst of the cold war.
His approach was so explosive,
his thighs like pistons propelled him
forward to rise sputnik-like in the air
and at the peak of his trajectory
he made a graceful turn
falling back to earth.
He became my model.
In grade 11 at the North York finals
I came second.

I remember the moment of looking at the bar
like an opponent,
almost as high as I was,
I visualized myself rising up to
and going over it,
the techniques, exact seven steps
in order to have the perfect turning,
then kicking the right barefoot straight
to high point in the sky
above my surroundings,
the hill, the tree
in preparation for this oh too brief flight.

I thrust my arms and body upward
higher than I've ever been
as if in a dream,
I'm flying above the bar
looking down on it
and I pause
in an instant brief as realization
that I know where I am,
more than any other time in my life
and then it was the turn,
that graceful parachute fall
back to earth.

Doug Kelman, Head Janitor of Emery C.I.

More of a friend,
he did not censor us as teachers.
Once in history portable
when I misfired a basketball and broke a window
the teacher, Mr. Laflair said: "Better go down to the janitor
and have him send somebody to clean it up."
When I confessed
Mr. Kelman raised his head puffed on his cigarette
"What window?"
But at the back of the school
he grilled Rolf and me,
"Can't you guys ever get here on time?"

He wore the custodial blue uniform,
always readjusting his tie
which never quite seemed to fit.
With his moustache resembled Trotsky
he acted often as a vaudevillian comedian,
making frequent jibes at the administration.
He was the alter-ego of the school.

In the early darkness of a winter afternoon
he would sweep with dust bane the school's debris
and later lower the flag and fold it.
Once a year in the war garden,
this navy sailor from the Second World War
would lay the wreathe
below the monument and the bell. Remembering.

The Poet

for Rolf Harvey

Swinging your trumpet from side to side
you strode down Habitant Drive singing
"For young Roddy McCorley goes to die
on the bridge of Toome today."
You made yourself out of struggle,
typing in the dungeon late into the night.
There you would sit by the redwood desk
under the painting of cabin in the Swiss Alps
with the old Royal typewriter with uneven keys
gleaming like an old altar
to write poems of invective and satire
metaphors darkly etched on onionskin paper.
You chronicled the pain of your mother,
your father, a handsome mustached gentleman in his sports coat
who played jazz in the big band in the thirties on the circuit
working now in the block house of Vicks VapoRub.
We read Cohen and listened to the raspy voice of Bob Dylan
on the Sea-breeze record player
or Rachmaninoff's "Rhapsody on a Theme of Paganini,"
the harsh beats evoking
the violinist's triumphant struggle with the devil
and the music rose before the dungeon's dark curtains.
We scribbled signatures
Karl Wolf, Mark Thorpe, John McCue on furnace pipes.
And I would walk home in my own snow soliloquies
with the wind whirling stories in their own currents,
watching my shadow grow in arched haloed light,
having before me the dark citadel of Emery
beyond the pines.

Writing

One night I heard the words, the music of words
I could see them on the page, I could hear my voice
and I understood what they meant.
The words brought the side of me which was hidden
and when I had finished writing the poem
it was dawn and the sunlight
was shining through the roses on the curtains.

Outside I walked down into the snowy ravine
and emerged into a field of light, the sky
with the red ribbed sand bars was like a sea
and I could hear the whistle of the train
and I felt that I could bring to life
everything in the world around me with words.

My father brought home an old Royal typewriter,
it could have been from the 1920's
with its high front like a forehead,
black as a model T car with the revolving ribbon,
the letters on the keys encased in silver rings
and I would punch them with my fingers
impressing meanings onto the textured page.

When I gave a sheaf of poems to my father,
he brought them back in a stapled book,
the poems in blurred brown ink
to hold in my hand…

History of Emery

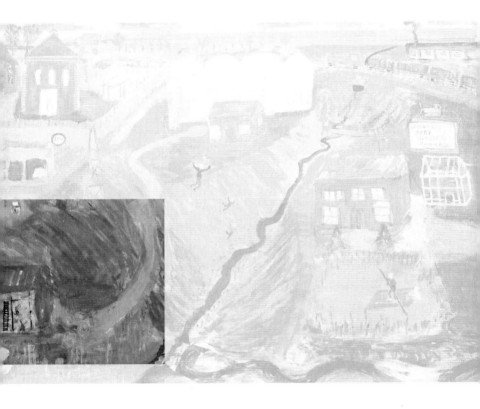

The Journey of Isaac Devins

Here I am an eighty-year-old man, thinking.
For the last time I survey the cabin,
the fields and hills of Emery,
the Humber Valley where I spent my life.
My wife, Polly calls out
"Isaac, you were never good at farewells."

We were here from the beginning.
I remember the years of war with America.
For weeks my father, Abraham, would be gone fighting,
mother and us children crammed into the smoky cabin.
We had no friends. Who were your friends?

The war dragged on and we began the long journey north,
we saw the British soldiers dead in the fields,
the lines of wounded prisoners.
With Governor Simcoe we crossed Ontario Lake
to safer British territory. When the fog cleared
we lifted our eyes to the unsettled shores:
this was to be our land.

So much to be done in those early months,
clearing the land at the mouth of the Don,
hacking out the bush for the Yonge Highway.
Elizabeth, our first child, was born in the Governor's tent.
Lady Simcoe said: "She is the first child born in the colony."

Nicholas and me built the King's Mill for the Governor.
We worked hard, hauling stone from the Humber River,
felling high timber from the smoky forests,
our horses grunting in the mud.

Aboriginals did not attack us,
only broke fences, stole wood.
The King's Mill rose like a tower,
the river turning the wheel into energy,
the grain into bread and whiskey.

I said goodbye to my father and brothers,
passing by the King's Highway, through Weston
we pushed our barge against late spring currents,
when it shallowed Elizabeth and Hannah jumped in.
Osprey and eagles swooped overhead,
the spawning salmon swished around us,
deer paused.

Rounding the bend I see my land,
the river, the tall stands of pine,
the sandbanks, hills that rolled.
Near the Oxbow I built my cabin.
My son James shared a plug of tobacco
with an Aboriginal chief,
he laughed at my jokes.
The river flows through the valley
past the ruins of the King's Mill.
I was miller, builder, surveyor, lumberman.
My sons and daughters will farm this land
for generations, as I have farmed I hope.
Polly is waving to me
—it is time to leave.

Simeon Devins Dying in a Tent
at Queenston Heights

My brother Levi has left me alone with the darkness,
shrapnel in my left side, my fever returning.
Last night we listened to the commotion of the river,
this morning when the mist lifted
the Americans were clambering up the slope.
When they drove us off the heights,
my militia unit was forced to regroup on the plain.
We were disconsolate until we heard
Commander Brock was riding down from Lewiston,
then like a fog broken by a beacon
he appeared and roused us—the great warrior charging
with us behind him up the rocky slopes.
Suddenly he recoiled, wounded,
but we charged on, chased the Americans from that bloody hill.
Later we learned our beloved Brock was dead,
he lies in the next tent, mourned.
This afternoon, I too was hit.
I know I will not recover.
I am delirious, drifting through a river of mist now
catching in memories my brothers:
Isaac salmon fishing on the Humber,
Levi sailing on Lake Ontario.
I shall never work my farm.
I shall never marry.
Abraham, father, I see you on your porch
receiving news of my death.
Do not grieve,
you shall live in our free country
and my brother Abraham,
lost somewhere in America.
I hear the distant Niagara Falls upriver,
$$\text{a final reckoning, I fear.}$$

Robert Grubb

They have renamed St. Andrews calling it Thistletown
—it sounds more like a weed than a town.
If father were alive today, he would be angry.
His legacy is beginning to fade.
I received one hundred pounds from his estate,
my brother received "Brae Burn."
That was not fortunate either.
Last year when it burned down
Whitrock and Eliza, my sister,
were lucky to escape with their lives.
The maid ran outside half "nakit,"
as Robert Burns would say, into the full daylight.
Far from Edinburgh or New York we must live.
On the edge of my father's account books,
outside the realm of his figures
I write about the love of dancing and a woman.

While father was alive,
there were never parties at the house on New Year's Eve,
but this last night the tables were set with
pâtisseries, hors d'oeuvres—delicacies of all sorts
and we danced until three in the morning.

Father's portrait still dominates the room.
Albion Road is falling into disrepair.
Grand Trunk is building a railway through Weston
and my father's company in due course will be bankrupt.
I am Robert, his eccentric son.
I write my poems on the margins of his life.

Clairvoyant

for Patty

There are some who say I'm a witch,
they avoid me as if I'm possessed,
afraid I'll determine something in their future.
When I'm silently rocking, speaking to myself,
I see things in the lightning of night clouds.
Last year I dreamed of rustlers and convinced the men
that we must stay up and we caught thieves like I said we would.

Don't ask me how it works,
how the moonlight falls just right in the field
where the rabbit sits vigilant in the grass,
the peculiar hush of wind on water announcing a storm.
I know it as I know the weave of my knitting.
I could see that the Devins' girl would drown in the pond.

They say I have healing hands,
they have power to let pain go.
I could tell them if they would listen.
I know that the heart hears its own blood beating,
as will has its own special warmth that can save you,
the pain leaves—you cannot fight the current.

I've sat up nights and felt myself whole as a landscape.
I think that there are dangers in the dark.
Even my husband, especially he, should believe in this power
but he is a man of few words who trusts his work
and what he can make with his hands.

My power comes from my secret knowing.
There are many things that men have to learn,
but they go on earning their living,
my living is already learned right here
rocking in my night chair,
seeing the dark side of the moon.

Reaman Castator Recounts Walter Lund Striking Out

It was so long ago, but I remember it as if it were yesterday.
At recess, and it was a recess like any other,
we were playing on the diamond, south of the school.
I was pitching.
I remember lobbing the ball a little high over home plate,
—not a bad pitch at all—mind you and Walter swung,
I could see the dazed look in his eyes
as the bat tumbled from his hands
and he staggered toward the school door,
falling on the cinders just beyond first.
There was no nurse in the school that day,
so leaping on my old Raleigh,
I headed for Will E. Duncan's farmhouse.
I passed the empty train station.
There was no one at home at Kaiser's or Riley's.
Pumping the pedals, swinging wildly from side to side,
with my temples pulsing
I charged into Will E.'s kitchen:
"Walter Lund's collapsed on the field.
He's breathing kinda funny."
Will E. grabbed a bottle of Five Star from the cupboard:
"Give him this while I go for the doctor."
The wheat fields in front of me
wavered in their full furnace heat,
my legs felt as if they were going nowhere
as if in a nightmare lost in time.
I swivelled through gravel, over the sticky tar,
my face running with sweat,
the gold stars quivering on my fingertips.
I see it now: the house, the station.

Bouncing high over the tracks,
I could see Walter lying there
surrounded by the kids.
I spun my bike and ran toward him,
lifted Walter in my arms,
poured the whiskey between his lips,
but they did not move;
it ran down the side of his mouth
and I knew he was gone.

Major "Lex" MacKenzie

As we drive past Wonderland
Jean Dalziel recalls Lex MacKenzie.
He was my uncle's brother,
the highway named after him.
As a boy he delivered goods for the Wallace brothers
driving the wagon early mornings down Albion Road.
During the First World War he fought
at the Battle of Vimy Ridge,
in the trenches his friend was killed
and he was shot in the arm,
(he had that arm in a sling for seven years,)
when he saw the sniper
Lex picked up the rifle and shot him.
He was a deadly marksman.
Later he went up north to join the Hunt Club
but he himself didn't hunt
couldn't shoot a deer.
He was the world's greatest storyteller.
You only believed a quarter of what he told you.

The House of Jean Agnew Dalziel

Off busy Steeles Avenue we enter the lane
and follow the winding path opening through the trees
into the old estate where you were born and got married.
Things look much as you left them when you
sold the property to Pioneer Village.
We walk up the wooden stairs.
In the bedroom you were born in, Jean,
the wallpaper is peeling,
a double mattress lined up against the wall.

In 1918 in the typhoid outbreak
your father was lying in the next room
and your mother who had typhoid too
was giving birth to you.
When the doctor was asked what should they feed the baby
he said, "Don't worry it won't survive."
You were only two and a half pounds,
they put you on the edge of a heated oven
burning one side of you,
but you survived.

Many years later at a golf club wedding
you said to this doctor:
"You don't look so well.
Can I do anything for you?"
"No, you aren't even supposed to be here."

At the end of a hall I see an old trunk
that came over with your great-grandfather.
On the ship he said:
"If you don't hurry up there will be no land left."
He got the land.

In the stillness of the afternoon
the village tractor cuts swathes through the tall grass.
You point out the Elizabeth tree by the barn
and I recall my hayride there in grade eight.
Now, the maple tree she planted is 40 feet tall,
with black tar on the bark.

"Elizabeth Arden promised us the moon
but didn't even give a star" you said.
The curator unlocks the door to the salon
where your father's Heintzman piano sits.
When the young Elizabeth Arden sang,
he would say, "Shut up, you Grahams can't sing."
This is the room of your ancestors,
your great grandfather marched with Mackenzie
up Yonge Street in 1837.
We leave the house, follow a path
and stop for a moment at the pioneer graveyard,
no larger than a small garden plot.

The Day Orrie Trueman Climbed
Emery Schoolhouse Tower

Charlie Grubbe and Aubrey Ella recall certain days:
the day teacher Macdonald shook Castator
until the nails came out of his desk,
the day that Walter Lund dropped dead in a baseball game,
and the day Orrie Trueman climbed the school bell tower.
Dared by the boys to ring the bell
he began to climb the bricks on the south side,
finding a foothold in the half-inch edges
and use them like rungs on a ladder climbed up into the sky.
As he climbs he could see
Art Peeler's dumbfounded face at the window,
his classmates getting smaller.
His climb would be something special:
something the boys would talk about,
maybe even the girls would notice,
something to give him a place in the school.

When Orrie finally stood on the rooftop of Emery
and rang the clapper, the village stopped.
Probably, his mother ran out of the kitchen door,
her tea towel wrapped around her wet hands,
his stepfather walked out of the barn and took off his hat,
Jennie Gillis stopped scattering grain to the chickens.
Below him the pupils shouted and whistled,
he heard the sound of the strap in the principal's voice,
but it didn't matter as long as he stood at the summit.
It made him forget about losing at soccer,
wearing the dunce cap.
Years later, when reveille awoke Orrie
and the sun glared down over the battlefield of the Sahara,
he stood again in the school tower and rang the bell over Emery.

The Stolen Photograph

When I visited Orval Parkes' mother,
I had wanted to show her the photo of her son's grave in Sicily.
I remember the night I found him.
It was humid and I had been off duty for the day.
There had been little shelling that night.
The spring was thick with the smell of orange blossoms.
I stopped to watch children drawing pictures in the dirt,
a crippled old man was throwing a bocce ball while others laughed.
I saw a *signorina* in a yellow dress looking at me.
As I made my way back to camp, my commanding officer yelled,
'You better come quick. Some of your boys took it hard last night.'
When the new dead were brought back was the worst time.
I saw them piled on the army truck.
Each man wore the pain of his own death.
The soldier with the disfigured cheeks
I recognized as Orval Parkes.
'You know him?' the officer asked dumbly.
Words made no sense to me then.
As I walked in silence down the farmer's road
by the brambled fence,
looking for any sign of mercy under that sick moon
all that I could think of was Orval at home:
playing euchre in the smoky community hall,
playing hockey on the clear ice at Emery,
dancing with the Woodbridge girls,
helping his father with the threshing.
The next morning, in that foreign soil, I buried Orval,
carving his name upon a cross of branches.
Under Mount Etna I took a photo of his grave,
but someone stole my camera the next day and I told her,
"I'm sorry I've nothing more to leave you, Mrs. Parkes."

Visiting Orrie Trueman at the Edge of Nobleton

1

The cicadas are buzzing in the still hot July afternoon
as I approach the shadowy bricked bungalow
and in the dark window, I read "Beware of Dog."
I ring the bell and wait until I hear shuffling footsteps
and a man with dishevelled grey hair,
dressed in an undershirt and loose trousers opens the door.

Earlier in the week I talked to Aubrey Ella, Orrie's stepbrother.
"His mother died in childbirth,
and as she was dying said to my mother:
'I want you to take my son.
I want him to keep his name, Orrie Trueman.'
Orrie's the one that thundered into the Board of Education meeting,
gave them hell and told them,
'You got to put the bell and the monument in the new school.'"

2

"I never want to see my grandchildren
go through what I went through," said Orrie.
"A lot of people think there's glory in it,
but brother, let me tell you
when you see the wounded brought in,
the young lads, seventeen, eighteen
just out of school… "

He remembers standing
in the desert night of El Alamein,
by his ambulance,
waiting for the planes to return,
hearing the throb of distant engines

and seeing the staggered formations of planes trailing
smoke through the sky.
His medical corps waited on the tarmac
while the planes landed.

They tried to get the wounded
and the dying onto stretchers,
injecting them with morphine,
talking to them,
dressing their wounds,
listening to their pain…
It continued for seven days
as if there were no night,
the sky breaking up in lightning,
the continual shrill scream of bombs.

3

"Do you know the men who were named on the monument?"
"There were Baggs in the neighbourhood who went to school
and Jeffreys was probably a hired hand."
"Who was Cecil Dodgson?"
"The Dodgsons lived in a log cabin where the school is now."
"Cecil Dodgson who was killed overseas in France?"
"Yes."
"Who was the last person who lived in the farmhouse?"
"I'm not sure.
Aubrey and I built that house in the 1930's."

Now I am back in the deserted house,
holding an oil lamp, stepping over a broken chair,
I open the old chest of war newspapers.
The screen door clacks in the cold autumn wind.
No more is this house a fiction of my mind.

Gladys Graham at Ravensbrück:
an Imaginary Letter to Elizabeth Arden

Dear Sister,
  You would not recognize me I have grown so gaunt,
my eyes hollowed, my lips cracked.
When my fingers grasp the barbed wire fence
I look to freedom beyond...
I watch the women walking aimlessly,
imprisoned for their resistance. I miss my life
mon mari, Paris, la langue française
—on fait des conjugaisons
je serai, tu seras, il sera
il n'y a pas d'autres choses à faire
ah, j'oublie, Florence
tu n'as jamais pu apprendre le français.
Ravensbrück is a horrible place,
guards with guns and hard faces.
Before the war in Paris at a dinner party
you called Herr Göring a fat pig.
How far you have come since the days
when we walked along the path from the log cabin in Emery
and you said: "I will be the richest little woman in the world."
Mais, c'était charmant, le petit Emery,
avec ses champs, ses collines et la Rivière Humber
et notre père qui parlait toujours de chevaux de race.
I had no choice. We could not let the allied pilots
be taken, had to get them back to England.
Sometimes, I think I'll go mad,
but you keep me sane, Florence.
There will be an end to this,
"Drink lots of water, flush out the poisons," you said.
So we have, and we will survive.
This letter will not leave my mind,
but know that I am well.
Someday, you will see I am alive.

Searching for the Log Cabin of Elizabeth Arden

What am I doing here at the edge of the city,
in the smoky heart of North York's industrial wasteland,
running across the highway ramp, and climbing
over the nine foot fence into a no trespassing zone?
Jack Devins said the "cosmetic queen" grew up in a log cabin
off the seventh and Jean Dalziel had pointed to these woods.

And here I am in a reedy swamp, pushing through
apple trees grown as thick as thorned limbs,
looking for any relic that might lead to her cabin.
The November night already closing in.
She was born New Year's Eve, 1879
on the Pine Ridge Road in the White Pigeon Hotel
and christened Florence Nightingale Graham.

Before me a pile of ruins, shattered concrete steps,
an RCA television set, a smashed Canada Dry tin,
a plastic chemical container with a fatal X.
I move on through pine trees to a broken cistern,
and reaching down I lift a concrete block
and inhale a scent of mint.

Here is the laneway where her father,
the huckster with his horse and wagon
would have trudged home with his wares.
I feel the fence with its splintered boards
bony as his stubborn Scottish fingers
and I imagine the old log cabin standing here.
She would have looked out upon this marsh
dreaming already of becoming Elizabeth Arden,
taking the name from Lord Tennyson's poem.
In her Fifth Avenue salon she would rememder this forest,

gazing at her Chagalls with their crazy steeples and flying cows,
recalled riding to Emery with her father on horseback,
seeing the ghostly Lawder giants returning from the mill,
hearing the teasing of the Castator boys,
smelling the horse manure from the Devins' stable,
skipping with Mary Hopcroft as the school bell rang.

She took her own name, Graham, for her stables.
Her horse, "Jet Pilot," prevailed, and she stood
in the winner's circle at Churchill Downs,
thinking of her father who raced thoroughbreds in Cornwall
to win his young bride over
before eloping to the end of the world.

Sometimes she would return to her Emery friends,
arrive at their farmhouses in a chauffeur-driven limousine.
At the opening of Black Creek Pioneer Village, her last visit,
her father's landlord, Mr. Dalziel, welcomed Florence.
"She is now Elizabeth Arden," whispered her secretary
"It's the first time I've seen Miss Arden cry."

Rowntree Mills Park

I remember in the Rowntree photograph the house
that overlooked the swift torrents of Hurricane Hazel.
Now I'm looking for signs of the house
that Joseph, the miller,
built for his family in the 1840's.
Below the roadway I follow this overgrown path
to the point where the house should be,
but there are only a few white stones
in the shape of a broken circle.

Farther along a square shaped stone lies
like a book in the earth.
The clear-etched stone points
to a fallen trunk, torn muscle striations,
a tree which may have sheltered the house.

Stop. Think. This is the place,
marked by smaller trees in the clearing overlooked by taller.
This is the house that Joseph Rowntree built,
the cornerstone he would have proudly set
at the ravine's edge overlooking the Humber.
Near a splintered trunk I kneel
and uncover a straight-edged stone
feel this stone, bone smooth,
pull away clinging moss,
tough sinews, rough roots,
this toughened old brick.

I walk to the edge of the promontory
and look across the river to the other bank,
to the line of mill workers' shacks
and I hear the saw tearing wood
at the lumber mill in North York.

At the grist mill on the Etobicoke side,
I can hear the paddling of the water
rushing through the mill course,
the regular sweeping rhythm of the wheel
and the turning levers and gears
at five in the morning.
I can imagine the flour rising through the moonlight
as the massive Lawder brothers heave
the barrels out into the waiting wagon,
hauling them down the rough clacking boards of Albion,
dreaming of the barmaids at the Peacock Tavern,
the barrels of whiskey at the end of the day.

My fingers dig among dried foliage and torn roots,
feel a twisted old ribbon of rusted metal,
a rim of one of the flour barrels.
Digging deeper I find another metal scrap,
a twisted water pipe from the house
along with the broken bottles of immigrant teenagers
who partied on these hidden foundations.

On the Way to Lindsay

1

Turn from the ramp to Toronto
and drive out toward Lindsay
to find the last Devins of Emery:
the direct descendant of Abraham and Isaac.
"Ray has the station sign," Marion Rowntree had said.

Through the ruins of farm machinery
the wind whines, blowing tumbleweed
across the Wagon Wheel Barn Dance Hall.
In the red Ford pickup he sits still,
his beard rugged and silver-flecked.
In the rough contours of his face I see
the Devins' lumbermen, blacksmiths, wagon makers.
"Been trying to shoot some deer this morning,"
he says, shifting his rifle over the gears.

2

"The Devins' book is wrong.
My mother didn't want anything to do with it.
Look inside the chest and bring me the blue box."
On the table I open it to the collection of war medals.
One of them a service medal from 1914-18
            for "Home and Country,"
a German Iron Cross,
                the Royal Canadian Dragoons decoration.
"There, Dad's medal of honour, right here."
"No," says Annis. "It's an essay prize for your mother, 1917."

One by one I touch the artefacts on the Devins' shelf:
the sharp blade of his father's bayonet,
his Uncle Roy's bootjack and spurs,
the refinished powder horn from Pennsylvania.
I recall Simeon dying in his tent after Queenston Heights,
John Chapman lying in the Toronto Jail after the Rebellion,
Levi's grandsons dying for the north in the Civil War.

"Do you have the Emery Railway Station sign?"
"Whatever we have is out in the Wagon Barn."
Annis leads me through the windswept yard,
across the grain of the deserted dance floor,
past the dumb turntables of the old recording studio
as the sweet dry smell of wheat hangs in the air,
         into the darkness of the barn
where sunlight flashes onto a hundred broken artefacts,
                              a museum storehouse.

Through the furniture we sift,
open the carriage maker's chest of shining tools.
I see these tools John Devins employed
to make the first Studebaker.
Annis uncovers an old commode,
"There it is. The sorting box of the Emery Post Office."
I look for lost letters of the Rowntrees and the Castators,
a letter that Jennie Gillis might have left behind
for Jim Macdonald or Pearl Usher,
but find only a mousetrap, old fuses,
         and a census in French and English for 1901.

There is no railway sign and I feel disappointed,
what remains of the Devins' and Emery's past
in the wagon barn
are old barley rakes, wooden wheels, worn saddles,
old tusks from an illustration of *King Solomon's Mines*,
the coloured drawings of Annis Saunders.

Listen, I can still hear the wind sifting the dust,
the rustling and jostling of couples
on Saturday nights, country and western dancing
singing of lost and found loves.
These are all the signs of Emery
        broken, and in their brokenness, whole.

                3

Annis leaves for the kitchen
while Ray leans over from his wheelchair.
"I used to steal kisses from the girls under the elms.
Many of the girls in Emery I had
out in the apple orchard
where I had a pup tent.
Don't ask who they were.
There are some things a man doesn't tell."

Mother and Daughter

What do I remember about Emery?
That was nearly forty years ago.
Yeah, we had good times.
There was always work to be done:
cutting the corn, mowing the hay, milking the cows...
you did that without complaining.
No, I got nothing more to say about Emery
Hurry up nurse, and finish my manicure.

Why would someone want to write about Emery?
I spent my life trying to forget the place.
That's all I have to say.
Why does a stranger call me,
dredging up the past.
My stepparents couldn't even bother
to show up for my wedding,
had to go to the Saturday market.
I would have done anything to get off that farm.
Never knew much good there anyway
except for the neighbour who I fell in love with,
left my husband and children for.
My chemotherapy starts Thursday
and on the weekend my daughter will be here
our relationship was not easy, you know.
  Oh, won't these fingernails ever dry.

The Deserted TTC Tram

On a cold February afternoon Les and I trudged through
the snow up the old farmer's road in Emery.
We saw the tram in the distance, so strange
in this farm setting like an old sailing vessel
anchored on the sea, while the wind blew
the spray of the snow across its dark face.

Through an open window we crawled inside.
The cold wind whistled through broken window panes.
The seats were replaced by shelves with boxes.
We opened one after another, held the decals in our fingers:
hockey players, football quarterbacks, Royal Canadian Mounties,
Aboriginals and rodeo cowboys on horses.
We had discovered treasure.

We stuffed quickly them into our pockets,
then decided to take the boxes and left
through the darkening landscape,
wadding through the deep snow.

In the springtime, a policeman arrived at our house.
"Someone has reported that you have decals on your bike.
Where did you get them from?"
My father stood with his arms crossed in the doorway.
The week before he had papered the spare room with them.

Now thirty-three years later, I ask Evelyn Thomas,
who was working for Mr. Storer.
 "Do you remember the tram?"
Yes, he kept his merchandise there."
"We stole some of those decals."
"It doesn't matter now," she said: "The street car burned down
a long time ago. Walt Disney has the copyright."

400 Drive-In

Beyond the farmer's field just below Highway 7
rose the giant slanted screen where father
would takes us in the old 58 Pontiac
up old Weston Road to the 400 Drive-In.
The block letters of the double feature were lit up
and my sisters dressed in their pyjamas
would run up to the playground
to swing and slide under the giant dancing
hotdogs and animated coca cola cups
until the first movie began.

From the slightly raised banks we watched
the family movies: *The Big Circus,*
the tightrope walker cross Niagara Falls,
Jason and the Argonauts
The war films: *The Bridge on the River Quai.*

One night with other boys we decided to sneak in,
we crawled through the woods past the lines of cars,
the pay booth and suddenly the guard
with a flashlight appeared,
"What the hell are you guys doing here?"
We began to run through the slippery gravel
past the cars with the teenage lovers
entwined before steamy dashboards,
past the surprised older couples who looked at us,
out beyond the lighted barge of the snack bar.

The guard chased us
and we running like soldiers
through a minefield in the war films
until the screen grew smaller diminishing into the sky.

And then were alone in the swamps with the frogs burping
and the crickets humming,
the bulrushes and the yellow flowers droop,
the night cool and misty around us
and the cars driving up the 400 like aliens.

Here I am again,
the farms and the forest are gone,
the gigantic star ship Cineplex Theatre
has replaced the Drive-In.
I walk right past the gate
with no attendant about to chase me.
I sit and watch the huge screen with the constellations
like that night long ago,
listening to the music of *Star Wars*
and the rolling of the credits.

On the way out I meet Helen
with thin grey hair
and watery eyes, missing a few teeth.
"Yes, I've been here since the theatre opened."
"Did you ever go to the Drive-In?"
"Yes, we drove up from the city with my family."
"Do you remember what movies you saw?"
"Nah, I can hardly remember yesterday."

Charlie Grubbe's Tour of Grouse Hill

Through the whispering grass we move.
   Charlie stops
     "Ah, what's this?"
Clearing the grass with his feet he finds a dip in the earth.
   "Around here about twenty feet from the river,
my father dug a well.
The hired hand, an Englishman, spent all one winter
digging a trench up the hill,
   in the spring the river
flooded the well and filled it up with salt.
We never found good water."

After Charlie Grubbe left, these ravines became mine.
I poled with the giant red haired boy across the pond.
I wandered like a vagabond among autumn hills.
I collected the oak leaves to press in Loblaw's book of knowledge.
I blew milkweed pods toward the mist-blown moon.
I was Dr. Leakey searching for Oulduvai man.
I was Robinson Crusoe stranded on Rabbit Island.
I was Superman flying from the high embankment.
I was Turok Son of Stone finding blind fish in sewer pipe caves.
I whirred through eons in H.G. Wells' Time Machine.

We move toward the mouth of Emery Creek.
   Across the river is the Grubbe homestead, "Brae Burn."
"There is an oxbow
       around here somewhere,
there were three on the deed.
     The mouth of the creek
should be just beyond
     the hill and tower

push this away…
        here we are.
                The Humber still has a good flow.
And there"
    he points to the ridge,
        "is the old road that led to the barn."

At the corner of Coronado Court Charlie stops the truck,
he recognizes a pine tree
        that stood at the gateway, two hundred feet from his house…
This is familiar territory. Gulfstream Public School
I trace my Globe and Mail *route,*
recalling the names… St. Lucie, Tampa Terrace
Azalea Court, Coral Gable and Gulfstream.
What mad developer had dreamed up these names?

This was Grouse Hill where the first school was built in 1834.
The barn was out there by Azalea Court.
Here the Griffith brothers built the Orange Lodge in 1845,
then it was turned into an icehouse.
A larger Home Circle Community Hall was built
then reassembled up at Emery
and finally at the end of the fifties
Kenny's father used the boards for a chicken coop in Milton.

The barn is here, where on a December morning in 1942,
George Grubbe (in the photograph a man holding a kitten
in front of the well and the icehouse)
was walking the bull in the barnyard
when something happened—either he had a heart attack or
slipped on a piece of black ice and when he fell the bull
stepped on his neck. Charlie heard him cry out,
carried him to the car and drove him to Humber Memorial
where on the operating table two hours later, he died.

It's the old red house like a phantom ship I remember
moored in the fog like one of Opa's old sailing vessels.
Before its facade I played my first game of pond hockey;
the blank half-deserted windows stared
as silent spectators from a lost legacy
while the Corrigan brothers, the big Swede and I
chased the elusive puck in the reed arena
where the ice as fast as silver glass was grained
with the scraping of our skates and Sherwood sticks
as we shot toward the rubber boot goal. It was so near, so far
as in the spell of the last winter we could not break.

Return to Emery

1

I remember the time when we moved in '56 to the old duplex
across from Masons, garage and diner,
where I first played in a poorly lit room
with a little cranky Dutch boy,
where the landlady said
that my mother opened the window so her canary flew away.

Lovilla Boulevard curves familiarly toward Weston Road.
The street had its own weather in different seasons.
Each house its own history.
Now the post-war houses are replaced.
How long it seemed to walk in Grade 3 to Melody Road School.
The school is gone now,
a flattened surface where
a new catholic school will rise.

2

The traffic is so busy
when we drive to the Crang's estate.
Across the road was a ranch style house
and a bomb shelter
built during the cold war.
Behind it I found antlers
in the forest of trilliums.
In this closest house to Crang's estate
John Bradley lived.
One warm autumn day we snuck up
inside the grounds,
crept by the hedge to view
the swimming pool then covered with leaves
but swirled with rumours of wild parties.

We traced our steps to the orchard,
climbed up into the trees
and were sitting up there
eating large yellow apples
when the man in a plaid jacket calls out,
"Enjoying the apples boys?"
It was the first time we were caught.
"Come on down now, run along
and take some apples with you."
As we walked away I turned to my friend,
"Do you know who that was?
It was Mr. Crang."

Now the door opens again
and I recognize the priest
from my previous visit with Tim Lambrinos.
He leads us into his living room and
speaks of the history of the house,
Percy Gardiner who made a fortune in metals in the '30's,
built it as a summer home
when it was still in the country.
Over the door the sign in Latin.
Unfortunate those who arrive and no one is home.

I ask if we can view Crang's Pond.
He leads us into a priest's room
with empty bookshelves.
"No one reads books anymore
it's a different world... digital."
He opens the curtains,
the spring light over the pond
illuminated it as an icon.

We walk down the steps to the place
where the swimming pool was.
It is a garden now, a shrine
where a young South American woman
is praying before a statue of Christ.

Slowly we cross the football field
for St. Basil's high school students
and try to find a way to Crang's Pond
but a row of tangled branches and dead trunks
along the shore prevents us from entering
until we find a gap.
The pond is smaller than it was
(formed in the 1950's
when gravel was taken from this quarry
for the new highway 401,
a nearby creek filled it up).

It was here below the Tudor mansion
that we played hockey games after school.
Sometimes, after the game I would put my Sherwood
down and skate across the glittering ice
over the dark underwater with sleeping reptiles,
the wild gold braids of weeds
like those of mythical girls…

3

Why am I standing again at the crossroads of
Finch and Weston Road thinking about the past?
So much has changed now.
Across the road was the old bricked house
that the Devins family once lived in.

(When it was abandoned
the house was used by drug dealers who squatted there).
Orrie Truman lived nearby.
I delivered *The Telegram* to him,
in the barn was the carriage maker's shop.

Aubrey Ella's house was across from the school,
he lived here until the end of the sixties.
From my math class I could see him harvesting
the oval tracks of the wheat field.
The Ella's farm was replaced by a large mall
which was demolished twenty years later.

Now, the Medallion Centre is being built
rising like a large ocean vessel
with new market square, boutiques, cafes
which will be full of new comers from different countries.

On the western side of Weston
was the old postal office
where Jenny Gillis was postmaster.
Later it became an Esso station
looking like a bunker with a grease pit.
From its machines we bought gumballs and peanuts.
The old community hall and Emery train station are gone.
It is a place of cargo containers and a scrapyard,
but soon an LRT will run across Emery.

This is the heart of Emery.
This is where the old school was
with the water pump,
near the pioneer cemetery that was moved to Woodbridge.
Now it's an Ultramar gas station.

4

Driving along Finch I see a variety of stores,
in place of Loblaws where I was
working as a stock boy is now
the Vietnamese Long Hui Supermarket.
At the end of Emery near Islington was Italian Gardens
with its pool, orchards, dance floor and racetrack.
Now is the Gordon and Irene Risk Community Centre
and the large hill with the Rowntree house is gone
only a small part of the embankment remains.
I see children play wearing Maple Leaf and Blue Jay caps
watched by women from the Middle East.
In this Italian neighbourhood,
the singer, Alfie Zappacosta grew up on Brubeck Road.

5

I remember that we could ride on Weston Road,
formerly Main Street on our bike treks
to Sportsland Park, the biggest swimming pool in the world
and you could go five minutes without seeing a car.
The roads are so busy as we pass The *Toronto Star* Press Centre
standing near its location,
and the 400 Drive-In became the Colossus Vaughan Cinemas.

6

There is one last place that I want to show Eva.
Across from the hill and Emery Collegiate
was the large forest of jack pine, white pine, spruce
that extended from Coronado Court
half a mile to Habitant Drive.
There before the high ridge, the Emery Creek

would have carved its course for thousands of years
undulating back and forth, past high cliffs of sand
gathering at places into ponds.

This is the place where I saw
the hawk glide and encountered a fox,
the artesian well in the log cabin,
a bridge above the trilobites in the bank.
I named this place Robinson Crusoe Island.
Now it is a construction site
(they plan to bring back here its natural beauty)
with over sized bulldozers,
the earth is hardened clay
like an old Roman road,
broken rock, gravel, muddy water.
What happened to the pine trees?
On the hillside the shrubs
tossed and turned
like the aftermath of a flood,
even the shape of the hills has changed.
The stream of coloured pebbles
is caged in a net of rocks
and the water does not have that old music.

I'm looking for something...
and when I see large spreading willow
I know where I am.
Here it is before me,
between the trees
no longer a road but a path,
a long green carpet of grass
reaching to the top of the hill.
This is the old farmer's road.

This is where our trips began,
where we climbed to the top
to see the old abandoned Usher barn.
This is where we heard
Johnny Wolf telling us about the decals,
this road that led us to the Storer's tram.
This was the land of Isaac Devins.

I call Eva to come
and standing on the ridge of the hill
I could see the expanded lines of the land,
Emery Collegiate on the summit
where the farm with the old trunks was,
the large pines before Habitant Arena.
This is the place I remember, my place
where the Humber River flows.

About the Author

Laurence Hutchman grew up in Emery, North York and attended Emery Collegiate Institute. He received his PhD at the Université de Montreal in 1988. He has taught at a number of universities including Concordia University, the University of Alberta, the University of Western Ontario, and the Université de Moncton, where he was a professor for twenty-three years.

Laurence Hutchman has published nine books of poetry, co-edited *Coastlines: The Poetry of Atlantic Canada* and edited a book of interviews called *In the Writers' Words: Conversations with Eight Canadian Poets.* He has received numerous grants and won awards including the WFNB's prize for individual poems, and in 2007 he received the Alden Nowlan Award for Excellence. He has served as Quebec and New Brunswick/PEI representative for the League of Canadian Poets and was President of the Writers' Federation of New Brunswick. Hutchman has given many readings and conducted numerous workshops in Canada, the United States, China, Ireland and Bulgaria. His work has been translated into French, Spanish, Dutch, Italian, Polish, Bangla and Chinese.

He lives with his wife, the painter and poet Eva Kolacz-Hutchman in Oakville.